Developing a Survey (Probability) Design to Evaluate the Presence and Distribution of Aquatic Invasive Species in Low Risk Waterbodies in the Greater Yellowstone Area

Natural Resource Report NPS/GRYN/NRR—2011/428

K.E. Griswold, Ph.D.

Idaho State University
Department of Biology
Pocatello, Idaho 83201

David P. Larsen, Ph.D.

Pacific States Marine Fisheries Commission
c/o US Environmental Protection Agency, Western Ecology Division
200 SW 35th St.
Corvallis, Oregon 97333

July 2011

U.S. Department of the Interior
National Park Service
Natural Resource Stewardship and Science
Fort Collins, Colorado

The National Park Service, Natural Resource Stewardship and Science office in Fort Collins, Colorado publishes a range of reports that address natural resource topics of interest and applicability to a broad audience in the National Park Service and others in natural resource management, including scientists, conservation and environmental constituencies, and the public.

The Natural Resource Report Series is used to disseminate high-priority, current natural resource management information with managerial application. The series targets a general, diverse audience, and may contain NPS policy considerations or address sensitive issues of management applicability.

All manuscripts in the series receive the appropriate level of peer review to ensure that the information is scientifically credible, technically accurate, appropriately written for the intended audience, and designed and published in a professional manner. This report received informal peer review by subject-matter experts who were not directly involved in the collection, analysis, or reporting of the data.

Views, statements, findings, conclusions, recommendations, and data in this report do not necessarily reflect views and policies of the National Park Service, U.S. Department of the Interior. Mention of trade names or commercial products does not constitute endorsement or recommendation for use by the U.S. Government.

This report is available from Greater Yellowstone Inventory and Monitoring Network (http://science.nature.nps.gov/im/units/gryn/) and the Natural Resource Publications Management website (http://www.nature.nps.gov/publications/nrpm/).

Please cite this publication as:

Griswold, K. E., and D. P. Larsen. 2011. Developing a survey (probability) design to evaluate the presence and distribution of aquatic invasive species in low risk waterbodies in the Greater Yellowstone Area. Natural Resource Report NPS/GRYN/NRR—2011/428. National Park Service, Fort Collins, Colorado..

NPS 960/108554, July 2011

Contents

Figures

Tables

Abstract

The Greater Yellowstone area is world renowned for its ecological importance and recreational opportunities. However, the area is threatened by aquatic invasive species. A multi-agency group, the Aquatic Invasive Species Subcommittee of the Greater Yellowstone Coordinating Committee (http://fedgycc.org/AISOverview.htm) identified inventory and field surveys to determine the presence and distribution of aquatic invasive species important to address this threat. The goal of this project is to design a monitoring program to estimate the presence and distribution of invasive species in the low risk waters of the Greater Yellowstone area using a survey (i.e., probability) design. Waters characterized as low risk are high elevation and relatively remote, as such they are seldom visited and have a lower risk of aquatic invasive species infestation than waters with heavy human use that are characterized as high risk. Waterbody types include streams, ponds, and lakes. Here, we propose a spatially balanced sample design that includes 20 sample sites per year for five years. We report relevant background information, the methods we used to develop the probabilistic sample design, a list of potential sample locations and sample site map, and our conclusions and future recommendations.

Acknowledgments

This work was supported by the National Park Service' Greater Yellowstone Inventory and Monitoring Network. The following members of the Aquatic Invasive Species Subcommittee (AISS) of the Greater Yellowstone Coordinating Committee contributed to the ideas and provided the background information for the sample design and provided editorial comments on this report: Susan O'Ney (Grand Teton National Park), Lee Mabey (US Forest Service Caribou-Targhee National Forest), Scott Barndt (AISS committee chair, US Forest Service Gallatin National Forest), and James Capurso (US Forest Service Region 6). Stephen Phillips (Pacific States Marine Fisheries Commission) provided helpful editorial comments.

Introduction

Background

In the western United States, federal and state land managers are charged with the stewardship of important ecological and cultural resources. These resources include remote, high elevation waters with relatively few human impacts as well as popular and large lakes that annually draw millions of visitors from around the globe. Some visitors bring unwelcome hitchhikers—aquatic invasive species that potentially threaten the native biota. If these species become established, they can displace native species and cause massive ecological (Vitousek et al. 1997) and economic impacts (Pimentel et al. 2000). Detecting and mitigating aquatic invasive species before they become established or spread is a standard approach for addressing their potential impacts. Thus, documenting their presence through field surveys and monitoring is an important component of any aquatic invasive species program.

The Greater Yellowstone area (GYA) is world renowned for its ecological importance and recreational opportunities. However, the area is threatened by aquatic invasive species. To address this threat, a multi-agency group, the Aquatic Invasive Species Subcommittee (AISS) of the Greater Yellowstone Coordinating Committee (GYCC) (http://fedgycc.org/AISOverview.htm), identified inventory and field surveys to determine the presence and distribution of aquatic invasive species (AISS Strategic Plan 2009; http://fedgycc.org/AISPlansReports.htm). The goal of the AISS is to develop a monitoring program within the GYA that will provide a means for early detection and rapid response to newly established populations of aquatic invasive species, or potentially reduce their spread if they are already established. In 2009, the AISS, along with experts in the field of aquatic invasive species, developed a framework for inventory and monitoring for aquatic invasive species within the GYA (McMahon et al. 2009). The participants proposed that the AISS develop a holistic monitoring program (not species specific) that used a stratified survey design for GYA waters. This program would comprise two components: (1) fixed locations that had a high risk of aquatic invasive species invasion that would be sampled annually and (2) locations with a lower risk of invasion that would be sampled on a less frequent basis. The locations identified as high risk are associated with high human use, and thus a higher number of potential vectors of invasive species. The second effort, the one we address in this paper, focuses on waters that are more remote, at higher elevations, and are impacted by fewer human vectors, potentially conferring a lower risk of infestation. The expert panel recommended developing a probabilistic sampling design for the low risk sites with a unique set of streams, rivers, and wetlands sampled each year.

Here, we report relevant background information, the methods we used to develop the probabilistic sample design, a list of potential sample locations and sample site map, and our conclusions and recommendations. Over time, the information gathered from the monitoring effort we propose will help us understand the extent of biological invasions by creating a scientific baseline that is representative of the low risk waters within the GYA. This is important, because while the risk of infestation may be low in these locations, the impact of a biological invasion would be high, as the potential for the invasive species, once introduced, to spread downstream is high. In addition, the sites identified as low risk are important ecologically and provide habitat to a disproportionate number of sensitive and threatened species (McMahon et al. 2009). In the AISS sample framework, low risk sites are at times described as "pristine" because of their remote location and limited access by humans. Here, we use the term "low risk." We believe the term is descriptive of the locations, yet does not require us to determine a priori if the location has been impacted by human activities, potentially including aquatic invasive species. While many of the sites are remote and should have fewer impacts relative to other locations, the sites may have undergone impacts of human activities such as mining, grazing, and climate change.

There are challenges to developing any monitoring program; in this case, they include the large land mass, waters in remote locations with little access, and a wide range of species that could potentially threaten GYA biota. Developing a coordinated effort that builds on the existing strengths of agencies, relies on existing sampling efforts and education are all part of the AISS strategy to face these challenges. Thus, one of the objectives of the newly developed monitoring program is that the new tools and approaches can be applied across landscapes and multiple jurisdictions without adding undue burdens on any given agency. Using a probabilistic sampling design is a useful approach because it establishes a sample design representative of the GYA.

Problem of aquatic invasive species

Aquatic invasive species are a major threat to biodiversity (Vitousek et al. 1997), and have been described as one of the most profound human impacts on ecosystems (Strayer 2010). Invasive species can alter food webs, displace native species, alter habitats, and introduce novel diseases. Human vectors are the primary source of biological invasions and areas of high human use are especially vulnerable (Vitousek et al. 1997). Boat ramps and rivers and streams with high angler impact are examples of locations within the GYA where the potential for human vectors is high (Gates et al. 2009). However, the establishment and impact of aquatic invasive species on native biota and landscapes is complex and can vary geographically (Ricciardi and Kipp 2008; Strayer 2010). Additional stressors such as climate change or landscape disturbance can affect the successful establishment and expansion of aquatic invasive species (Rahel and Olden 2008; Lee et al. 2008; Bierwagen et al. 2008). For example, temperature changes are likely to change the elevational distribution of native and nonnative species. The proposed monitoring in GYA waters will document the current status of waters (infested or non-infested) and in the future may allow for the detection in changes in distribution and abundance of invasive species (McMahon et al. 2009). This will improve our understanding and help managers address the dynamic nature of biological invasions as the impacts of climate change effect the area, an objective identified by the AISS expert panel (McMahon et al. 2009).

There are several monitoring programs currently in place in the GYA. In some cases, the focus is a single species, in others, the effort focuses on documenting a broad number of species. For example, interagency efforts that focus on native cutthroat trout species are in place within the GYA and are administered by a number of agencies and cooperative efforts (see May et al. 2007 for an example). Documenting nonnative salmonids that displace or hybridize with native cutthroat trout has been a part of this program for over a decade (May et al. 2007). Holistic sampling efforts (e.g., those that focus on broad spectrum of species), include monitoring by the US Environmental Protection Agency's (EPA) Environmental Monitoring and Assessment Program (EMAP) and Portland State University (see McMahon et al. 2009 for a more thorough review of GYA monitoring). Integrating the current effort with existing efforts, including data sharing, was identified as a priority by the GYA AISS.

The aquatic invasive species that potentially threaten the GYA include a number of bivalves, fish, macrophytes, plants, disease pathogens, crustaceans, amphibians, reptiles, and mammals (McMahon et al. 2009). Currently, invasive species including lake trout (*Salvelinus namaycush*), brook trout (*Salvelinus fontinalis*), rainbow trout (*Oncorhynchus mykiss*), brown trout (*Salmo trutta*), New Zealand mudsnails (*Potamopyrgus antipodarum*), and whirling disease (*Myxobolus cerabralis*) are present within the GYA. The diatomaceous algae, "Didymo" (*Didymosphenia geminata*), grows in large blooms and creates a spongy mat on stream bottoms, is considered native to the region, but there is concern about increased nuisance blooms and transport of the organism via anglers to other locations.

Developing the response design, or specific sampling protocols, is outside the scope of this study, but is detailed in McMahon et al. (2009). In that report, they developed a focal list of invasive species, but they also recommend that sample surveys would be more efficient and in the long run more useful, if they resembled a biological survey that documents native and nonnative species.

Probability Based Sample Design

Overview and sample design goals

As introduced in the background section of this document, the goal of this project is to design a monitoring program to estimate the presence and distribution of invasive species in the low risk waters of the GYA using a survey (i.e., probability) design. Science-based monitoring programs are designed around a statement, or series of statements of interest that address particular objectives (Downes et al. 2002). The results should be simple, clear and, in the case of the GYA, something that can be communicated to a wide variety of audiences. Our approach is patterned after the "monitoring wheel" first presented in Ward and Peters (2003) and recently elaborated at www.salmonmonitoringadvisor.org. In this document, we address the first two components of the monitoring wheel: (1) goals and objectives; and (2) spatial and temporal design. Other components of the monitoring wheel include data collection, data management, interpretation and reporting, and finally, design revision. These elements are outside the scope of this report, which is restricted to identifying a suite of spatially balanced sample sites; however, as the project moves forward they will need further development.

One of the most important aspects of the first step of the monitoring wheel is to define objectives in sufficiently clear terms that a spatial and temporal design can be implemented to achieve those objectives. To adequately define the objectives the introduction of some terminology is required:

Target Population: The target population describes the "entity" that will be described by the results of the monitoring program. The target population can be discrete, such as all lakes in a region of interest; or continuous, such as a road network in a state. The target population includes the set of all the units or elements for which inference is intended and should directly reflect the monitoring activities.

Sampling Frame: A sampling frame is a representation of the target population, as complete collection of all possible sample units from which a census can be conducted or a sample can be drawn. For natural resources, the sampling frame is usually a digital representation of the geographic location of the units or elements of the target population such as a stream network or the geographic location of lakes and wetlands.

Sampled Population: The sampled population represents the actual population that is sampled. Ideally, the sampling frame, sampled population, and target population are the same. However, sampling frames are generally not complete, or contain errors, and the sampled population might exclude parts of the sampling frame due to, for example, denial of access to some sites, or sites might be too remote or dangerous to sample.

Probability-based sampling: Although monitoring the entire target population might be desirable (i.e., conducting a census), conducting a census is rarely affordable. A method that incorporates randomization in sample unit selection (called probability based sampling, EPA http://www.epa.gov/bioiweb1/statprimer/probability_based.html) is often used to select a representative sample on which measurements are made and inferences developed to estimate the condition of the target population. This randomization ensures a reduction in potential bias from judgment or convenience sampling, thus increasing the validity of extending inference from a sample to the population of interest.

One of the challenges in developing probabilistic sample design and understanding the inference for reporting is identifying the target population. Sample design implies that we take a sample of "something." That something is the "target population" represented by a "frame." In a sense, the probability sample selects a "miniature" of the target population, takes measurements on that miniature, then makes inferences to the target population (Tony Olsen, US Environmental Protection Agency, pers. comm.). So, defining the target population in a way that both allow us to select a sample and to use the measurements on the sample to make inferences about the target population is crucial. If we cannot define the target population and represent it as a frame, we cannot generate a sample of it.

An additional desired characteristic for monitoring natural resources is to represent the spatial pattern in resource characteristics. Stevens and Olsen (2004) developed an algorithm that incorporates both randomization and spatial balance in the selection of a representative sample of sites to meet this need, called Generalized Random Tessellation Stratified (GRTS) design . GRTS is highly flexible, allowing sample stratification, or replacement of samples (preserving the spatial balance) if, for example, access is denied, or samples cannot be obtained or other reasons The approach is useful in real world settings where access and remote sites may limit sampling opportunities, such as in the GYA. It differs from simple random sampling in that it is less likely to create clusters of sites or gaps in site locations. It is more flexible in meeting sampling needs for natural resources than systematic designs.

Spatially balanced designs, such as GRTS sampling, can be used to address questions regarding the status and trend of biological or habitat indicators in aquatic ecosystems. Status, in the broad sense, is simply the state or condition of a parameter such as distribution or abundance and can be described as a snapshot in time, while trend quantifies change over time. Robust estimates of regional status require a large number of sample sites over a broad spatial extent. Detecting trend improves by repeated sampling over time often over long time periods since natural variation in the environment can obscure the detection of trend (Larsen et al. 2004). When designing surveys of natural resources the balance between estimating status or trends, the allocation of sites to achieve status (more different sites) or trend (returning to the same sites) objectives must be evaluated. This requires evaluating the effects of spatial and temporal variability of the indictors chosen for monitoring on status and trend estimates.

Objectives
To identify the objectives of the project we conducted a series of conference calls and email correspondence. The following project objectives were identified:

1. define the target population for aquatic invasive species monitoring in the GYA;

2. identify the sampling frame that best represents the target population;

3. develop candidate probability designs;

4. select a design that can meet the primary monitoring objectives within the budget constraints;

5. select a sample of sites to be monitored;

6. report on the process, findings (including sampling sites), and recommendations for future work; and,

7. identify and address additional sampling issues to refine spatial, temporal, and response designs (if additional funding is available).

To meet these objectives, the group examined a series of data "mock-ups" and sample design scenarios for evaluation. Revision to mock-ups or re-examination of reporting objectives and scope of inference was conducted through email correspondence or phone discussions.

In addition to the project objectives listed above, The Salmon Monitoring Advisor (www.salmonmonitoringadvisor.org) suggests that an explicit objective statement for monitoring include the following components (refined by Tony Olsen, US Environmental Protection Agency, pers. comm.). The components of the objective statement were based on McMahon et al. (2009) and refined through conference calls and email correspondence. They reflect the scope of the current agreement and include:

Target Population: All perennial, low risk waterbodies within the GYA. Waterbodies include perennial streams/rivers and lakes/ponds.

Spatial Domain: GYA as defined by the digital map shown in Figure 1. (Virginia Kelly, Greater Yellowstone Coordinating Committee, provided shape files that bound the geographic area of the GYA to develop this map.) The GYA includes Yellowstone and Grand Teton National Parks, parts of Idaho, Montana and Wyoming, and six national forests (Caribou-Targhee, Beaverhead, Gallatin, Custer, Shoshone, and Bridger-Teton), and the US Fish and Wildlife Service National Elk Refuge.

Spatial unit: Low risk waterbodies are defined as individual lakes, ponds, and stream segments within the spatial domain.

Temporal domain: Five years beginning in 2011. The planned duration of the study is five years; the duration can be easily extended using the same sample selection routines, or can be modified to address specific aspects of the currently defined target population.

Temporal unit: Year (i.e., sampling will be conducted during specified intervals each year, and annual summaries of results produced).

Based on these components and the overall goals and objectives, we developed the following objective statement:

> *Estimate the proportion of perennial, low risk waterbodies within the GYA that are free of invasive species in each of five years, and cumulatively over five years. Identify the locations of sampled waterbodies that contain invasive species.*

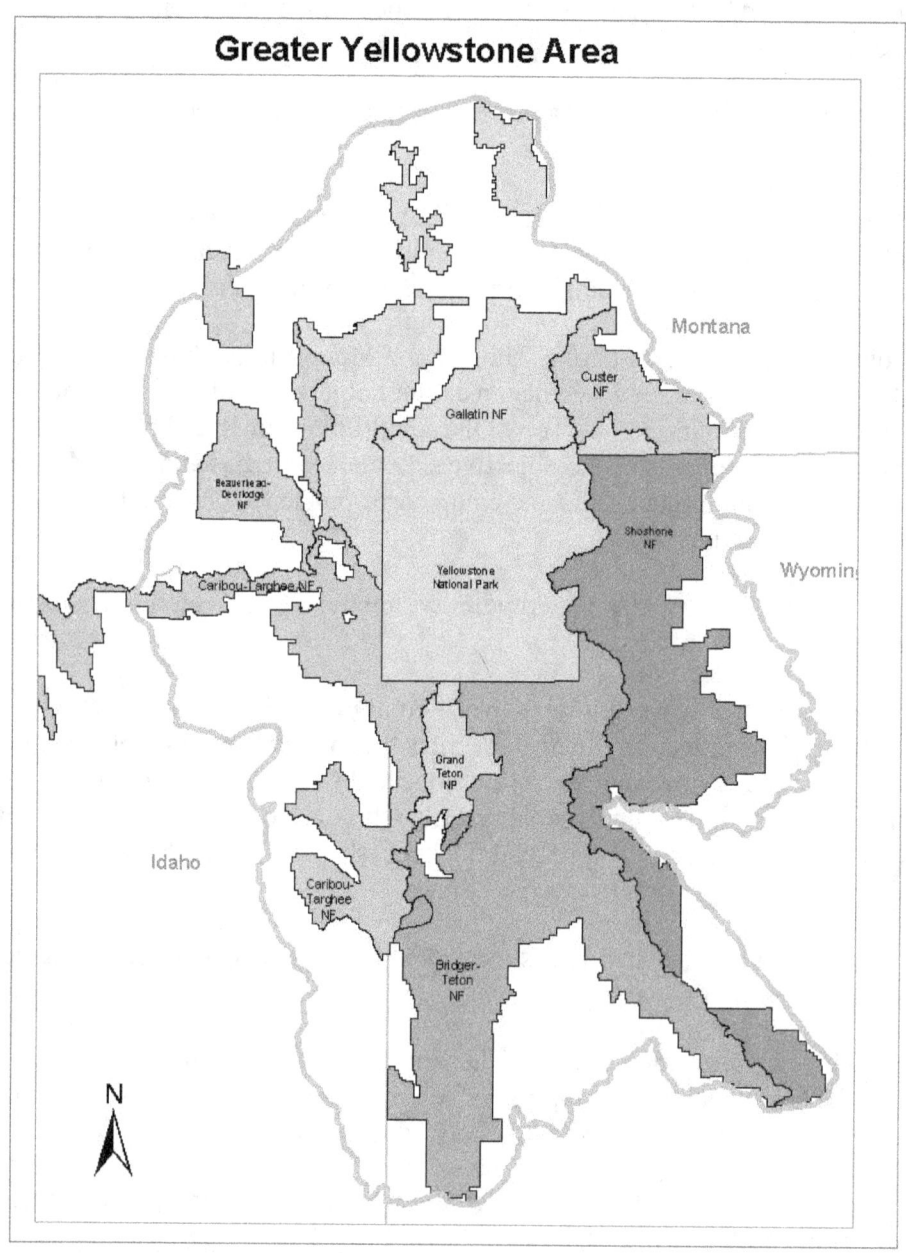

Figure 1. Greater Yellowstone Area sample domain developed using Geographic Information System (GIS) shape files outlining the geographic boundary and depicted by the green line. Jurisdictional boundaries are present where available.

Development of Sampling Frame and Survey Design

To develop the sampling frame, we first examined the availability of digital representations of waterbodies within the GYA. Stream, lake and pond coverages at both the 1:24 K and 1:100 K scale are available. We compared 1:24 and 1:100 K maps (from the National Hydrography Dataset [NHD+]) from different locations within the GYA to identify the resolution in digital maps that best represented the target population (for streams, lakes, and ponds). Based on our discussions and evaluation, 1:100 K maps (NHD+) best represent the stream and lake/pond target population. 1:24 K scale maps included lateral and ephemeral streams that were outside the area of interest of AISS biologists. Wetland delineation from the National Wetlands Inventory (NWI) is also available (original data was collected at the 1:64 K scale within the GYA). However, as noted below, resources available to this project were insufficient to compile a GYA wide wetlands frame from the NWI inventory. Consequently, NWI defined wetlands are excluded from the current design.

We then examined the US EPA's frame that it used as a basis for its National Aquatic Resource Surveys. Those surveys included separate frames for lakes, streams and rivers, and wetlands. For each survey, the EPA created separate sampling frames. For lakes, streams, and rivers, it refined the NHD+ digital hydrography based on the United States Geologic Survey (USGS) 1:100,000 scale digital maps, excluding a series of obvious errors in the files. The stream-river component could be sampled as a continuous resource, or as discrete waterbodies defined by segments. Although the EPA used the continuous representation for their sample selection, the AISS decided to define the stream network as discrete stream segments (as specified within NHD+), with a point location for each segment. The lakes component was refined from the "polygon" coverage within NHD+, with a point location (centroid) of each polygon specifying the geographic coordinates of lakes/ponds. The operational sampling frame is a "list" frame of the point locations of each stream and lake/pond in the EPA "cleaned" version of NHD+ clipped to the GYA boundaries. This frame contains a series of waterbody attributes including: (a) size (e.g., area for lakes/ponds; length for stream segments; (b) type (e.g., stream, river, lake, pond, canal, and perennial/intermittent status) designated by FCODE (a five digit code provide with NHD+ that describes the waterbody type). The specific sampling frame for the GYA consists of the xy coordinates for each stream segment and polygon with FCODE = 46006 (perennial stream reaches) and FCODE = 39004 (perennial lakes and ponds). The proposed sample frame was reviewed by AISS members at their annual meeting.

Part of developing a monitoring program requires recognizing various external constraints such as the potential budget. Although it is desired that uncertainty be expressed as a goal, budget constraints often limit the precision of the actual results. The key budget constraint for this monitoring program is mostly likely the hiring of additional field crews to conduct field sampling and therefore a reasonable number of field sites must be proposed. We propose that 20 low risk water bodies should be sampled each year for five years.

Options considered and design selected
We proposed the following different temporal and spatial sampling scenarios and their potential outcomes for consideration by AISS members.

9

1. Each year use a different set of GRTS selected sites from the target waterbody population of size N. Include an "oversample" that lists replacement sites to be used if any on the original list cannot be sampled (e.g., access denied, part of high risk sample, unsafe location due to slope, bear activity).

2. Similar to (1), but stratify the selection to select a greater proportion of lakes/ponds than stream reaches.

3. Similar to (1), but balance the sampling across sizes to get a greater number of larger lakes/ponds and reaches. For reasons discussed below, the distribution of samples is heavily skewed toward the small waterbodies.

4. Select a proportion of sites that would be resampled every year (or on some cycle such as every two or three years). The advantage of revisiting sites is that it gives greater trend detection power over a no revisit pattern.

AISS members identified Option 1, with a sample size of 20 waterbodies each year, which is the sample design that requires visits to unique locations each year. The results of this sample design would be simple to describe. Essentially, reporting would consist of the number of, or percent of waterbodies where invasive species were observed; this could be split into the two types: lakes and ponds; stream/river reaches. These summaries could be reported year-by-year as annual monitoring progresses, or could be cumulative such that after five years, a summary or "five year" statement about number or fraction of waterbodies where invasive were observed could be reported. Uncertainty of the estimate will be related to both the number of waterbodies sampled and the proportion with invasive species, so accumulating over time will decrease uncertainty of estimates. Mapping of sample locations annually where invasive species were found would help determine if there is a spatial pattern to the "hits," or detections.

An R-coded "grts" function was used to select 20 sites (along with an oversample of 20 sites) in each of five years (Figure 2). The R-code used is part of the Spatial Survey Design and Analysis software included in the "spsurvey" (spatial survey) library (available through www.epa.gov/nheerl/arm). The excel file "GYA_Sites.20 for five years with oversample" is available as a supplement to this report by contacting the authors and includes a number of self-explanatory fields for the site location including waterbody type, coordinates, oversample location, FCODE, Hydrologic Unit Code (HUC) number etc.

The list of sites that GRTS generates is in an order that preserves spatial balance across the spatial distribution of the frame. For example, the first ten sites are spread across the distribution of waterbodies in the GYA; the next 10 interpenetrate (i.e., fit within the spatial pattern of the first ten sites), to maintain a spatial balance across the 20 sites (Figure 2). Each year's sites also interpenetrate such that the 100 sites across the five years are spatially balanced. The oversample each year is also interpenetrating; this allows replacement of sites that might not be sampled in each year's list of 20 sites. For example, access to a site might be denied by a landowner. Each year's oversample should be used in its order. If one site is dropped from the list of 20, select the first site of the oversample for that year; if two sites are dropped from the original list, select the first two from the oversample, etc.

It is expected that a table similar to Table 1 would be used to summarize each year's results and cumulatively over the five-year study:

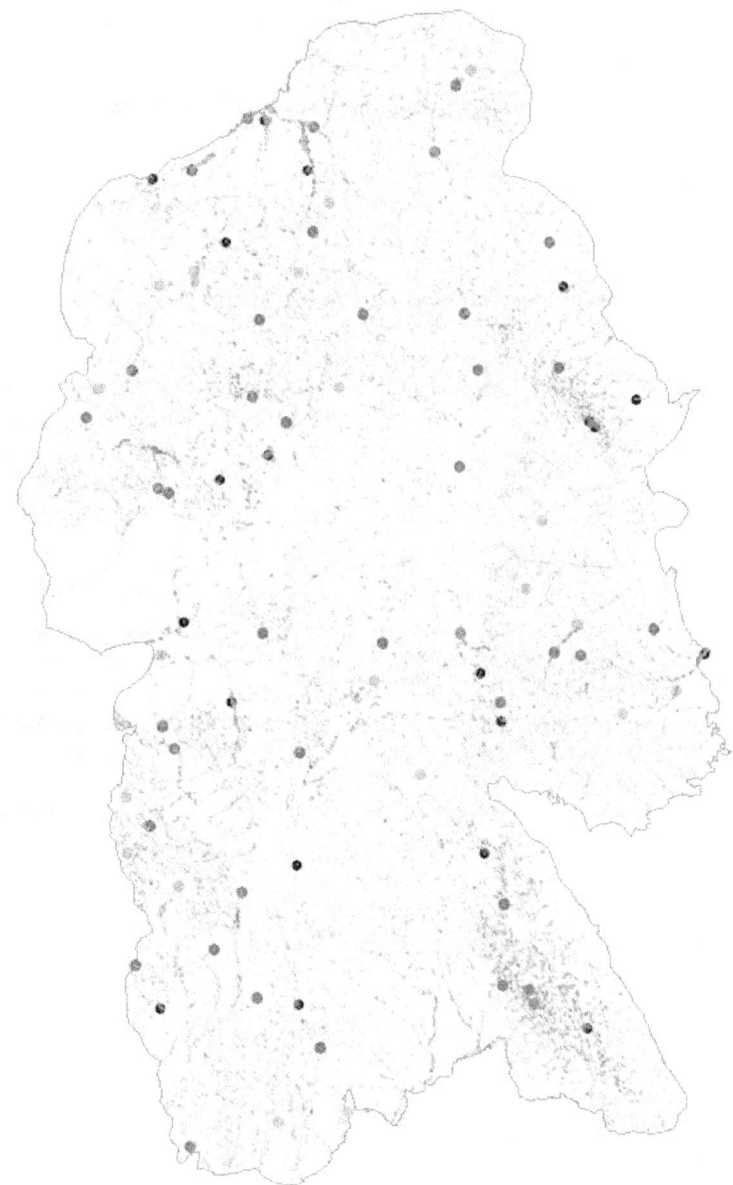

Figure 2. A map of 100 sample locations color coded by year (N = 20 per year) selected through Generalized Random Tessellation Stratified sampling for the Greater Yellowstone Area. Associated information for the points are provided in an excel file "GYA_Sites.20 for five years with oversample".

Table 1. Hypothetical results and reporting following each year for five years of sampling for AIS in Greater Yellowstone Area "low risk" waters.

Example Summary	Streams	Lakes and Ponds	All GYA "low risk" Waters
% free of ANS (2011)	70 % (n=x) (+/- x% CI)	80 % (n=y); (+/- x% CI)	73 % (n+x+y+z) (+/- x% CI)
% free of ANS (2012)	Etc.	Etc.	Etc.
% free of ANS (5-yr summary)	Etc.	Etc.	Etc.

Note: Well-designed probability surveys allow estimating of sampling uncertainty. Application of the GRTS algorithm allows the use of two approaches for estimating sampling uncertainty, one based on independent random sampling (i.e., no spatial balance in the selection of sites; Horwitz-Thompson), the second using a "local variance estimator" (Stevens and Olsen 2003). In situations where spatial patterns in the response are present, the Horwitz-Thompson uncertainty is biased high; the local variance estimator provides an unbiased estimate. Both methods are available in the spsurvey package using the function.

An approximate estimate of the uncertainty can be calculated from the formula (e.g., Snedecor and Cochran 1978):

$$\text{Stand error of proportion} = [(p*(1-p))/n]^{1/2}$$

Where p is the proportion estimated and n is the sample size. For example, the 95% confidence interval (+/- 1.96 times the s.e.) for an estimated proportion of locations without invasive species = 0.75 is +/- 0.19 for a sample size of 20, and +/- 0.08 for a sample size of 100. This estimate of uncertainty assumes that the evaluation of lack of invasives is accurate, i.e., no false negatives. There is a large body of literature that evaluates the role that detection probability plays in evaluating presence/absence. Evaluating detection probability usually requires repeated sampling of individual sample units, and a variety of approaches have been developed to correct for, or incorporate detection probability into estimates of presence or absence (MacKenzie et al. 2002, 2003, 2005). This aspect of uncertainty is not considered as part of this study, and is discussed below.

Discussion

For the sample locations we present (Figure 2), we did not stratify by size for either stream reaches or ponds and lakes. Because of the dendritic pattern of streams on the landscape, high elevation headwater streams are more prevalent, and will be represented in the probability-based sample proportional to their occurrence on the landscape. However, this outcome may be beneficial to the monitoring objectives of the AISS, as low risk, high elevation headwater streams are one of the target populations. In addition, there is about an order of magnitude more stream reaches than lakes and ponds within the GYA. So, streams will be included more often than ponds and lakes. Again, because the AISS is interested in holistic sampling, the proportional inclusion of ponds and lakes is a desired objective. Similar to stream reaches, small ponds and lakes will be represented proportional to their occurrence on the landscape, again a feature that allows the AISS to sample their target population. However, GRTS allows using an adaptive approach, so that stratifying samples by size can be incorporated at a future date if necessary. For example, if the sample includes stream reaches that are too small to accomplish the tasks in the response sample design it may be necessary to stratify by size to include larger streams.

The advantage of revisiting some sites on an annual or less frequent but regular basis is an increase in the likelihood of detecting a trend if a trend is present, but at the cost of visiting new sites. The outcome is a trade-off between potentially increasing the likelihood of detecting trend with an increased uncertainty about the fraction of waterbodies with invasive species. The sample design we present visits new sites each year, and therefore will not be as sensitive to trend detection as a design that includes revisits to sites over time. We suggest that after five years, the AISS revisit their sampling objectives within the context of their baseline data set and evaluate if trend detection is needed and feasible.

We emphasize that this document describes a method to select locations at which to conduct an evaluation of presence/absence of invasive species. It does not address the methods or protocols by which detection of invasive species at a site will be evaluated. The example (Table 1) that illustrates how summaries of proportion of waterbodies without invasive species could be presented does NOT include a correction for detection probabilities, or false negatives. Detection probabilities express the likelihood that a species is detected if it is present, hence affects statements about the proportion of the resource estimated to be free of invasive species. A large body of research has developed methods by which to estimate detection probabilities (MacKenzie et al. 2002, 2003, 2005; Harvey et al. 2009). The process involves repeated sampling of a set of sites during the sampling season to determine the frequency at which target species are detected. This detection frequency is then incorporated into an estimate of extent of invasive species. It is unlikely that resources are available to evaluate detection probabilities for the low risk aquatic waterbodies, partly because of the expense of getting to the remote sites. However, it might be feasible to evaluate detection probabilities at high risk waterbodies by repeated sampling of these during the sampling interval and use these detection probabilities as a first cut estimate of the detection probabilities for the low risk waterbodies. This could provide an indication of the potential error in the status estimates and support decisions whether to conduct an evaluation of detection probabilities for this group of waterbodies. Because developing detection probabilities is a complex process we suggest that the AISS's further work be conducted in collaboration with researchers at US Geologic Survey Patuxent Wildlife Research Center (http://www.mbr-pwrc.usgs.gov/software/presence.html).

Recommendations for Future Work

We anticipate that there will be challenges in determining the exact location for sampling activities or the sample unit. "Rules" for determining the locations should be developed such as: "stream sampling locations will be located 10 meters above the nearest downstream confluence with another waterbody" or "lake sampling locations will be located at or slightly above the lake outlet." However, because there is large number of target species with a wide range of potential habitats at the local or site specific scale, it may be necessary to consider the response design in terms of sample unit, and training field crews to determine the sample location will be required.

Once the sample design is implemented we suggest the AISS consider two additional approaches if funding is available:

- Develop a list of samples locations based on GRTS that target wetland habitats within the GYA. The wetland delineation from the NWI (original data was collected at the 1:64 K scale within the GYA) could be used as the target population within the existing GYA sample frame developed for stream and lakes.

- If invasive species are detected we suggest implementing an adaptive sampling regime in nearby waterbodies. For example, if an invasive species was detected at a sample location, sampling could be intensified within the affected waterbody (in stream, reaches above and below the affected area) and to adjacent locations (nearby lakes connected by a trail system, for example) to determine whether additional waterbodies were also inhabited by invasive species.

References

Bierwagon, B. G., R. Thomas, and A. Kane. 2008. Capacity of management plans for aquatic invasive species to integrate climate change. *Conservation Biology* 22:568–574.

Downes, B. J., L. A. Barmuta, P. G. Fairweather, D. P. Faith, M. J. Keough, P. S. Lake, B. D. Mapstone, and G. P. Quinn. 2002. Monitoring ecological impacts concepts and practice in flowing waters. Cambridge University Press, New York, New York, USA.

(EPA) Environmental Protection Agency. 2002 Aquatic resources monitoring http://www.epa.gov/nheerl/arm/designing/design_intro.htm (accessed 22 June 2011).

Gates, K. K., C. S. Guy, and A. V. Zale. 2009. Angler awareness of aquatic nuisance species and potential transport mechanisms. *Fisheries Management and Ecology* 16:448–456.

Harvey, C. T., S. A. Qureshi, and H. J. MacIsaac. 2009. Detection of a colonizing, aquatic, non-indigenous species. *Diversity and Distributions* 15:429–437.

Larsen, D. P., P. R. Kaufmann, T. M. Kincaid, and N. S. Urquhart. 2004. Detecting persistent change in the habitat of salmon-bearing streams in the Pacific Northwest. *Canadian Journal of Fisheries and Aquatic Sciences* 61:283–291.

Lee, H., II, D. A. Reusser, J. D. Olden, S. S. Smith, J. Graham, V. Burkett, J. S.Dukes, R. J. Piorkowski, and J. McPhedran. 2008. Integrated monitoring and information systems for managing aquatic invasive species in a changing climate. *Conservation Biology* 22:575–584.

Mackenzie, D. I., J. D. Nichols, G. B. Lachman, S. Droege, J. A. Royle, and C. A. Langtimm. 2002. Estimating site occupancy rates when detection probabilities are less than one. *Ecology* 83:2248–2255.

MacKenzie, D .I., J. D Nichols, J. E Hines, M. G. Knutson, and A. B. Franklin. 2003. Estimating site occupancy, colonization, and local extinction when a species is detected imperfectly. *Ecology* 84:2200–2207.

MacKenzie, D. I., J. D. Nichols, J. A. Royle, K. H. Pollock, J. E. Hines, and L. L. Bailey. 2005. Occupancy estimation and modeling: inferring patterns and dynamics of species occurrence. Elsevier, San Diego, California.

May, B. E., S. E. Albeke, and T. Horton. 2007. Range-wide status of Yellowstone cutthroat trout (*Oncorhynchus clarkii bouvieri*). Montana Department of Fish, Wildlife and Parks, Helena, Montana.

McMahon, R., S. Kumar, M. Sytsma, R. Hall, D. Britton, S. Spaulding, E. Williams, A. Farag, S. O'Ney, and J. Capurso. 2009. AIS Inventory and monitoring framework for the GYA. Available at http://fedgycc.org/AISOverview.htm (accessed 22 June 2011)

Olsen, T. 2008. Personal communication. Environmental Protection Agency. Corvallis, Oregon.

Pimentel, D., L. Lach, R. Zuniga, and D. Morrison. 2000. Environmental and Economic Costs of Nonindigenous Species in the United States. *BioScience* 50:53–65.

Rahel, F. J., and J. D. Olden. 2008. Assessing the effects of climate change on aquatic invasive species. *Conservation Biology* 22:521–533.

Ricciardi, A. and R. Kipp. 2008. Predicting the number of ecologically harmful exotic species in an aquatic system. *Diversity and Distributions* 14:374–380.

Snedecor, G. W., and W. G. Cochran. 1978. Statistical Methods. Sixth edition, ninth printing. The Iowa State University Press, Ames, Iowa, U.S.A.

Stevens, D. L., Jr., and A. R. Olsen. 2003. Variance estimation for spatially balanced samples of environmental resources. *Environmetrics* 14:593–610.

Stevens, D. L., Jr., and A. R. Olsen. 2004. Spatially-balanced sampling of natural resources. *Journal of American Statistical Association* 99:262–278.

Strayer, D. L. 2010. Alien species in fresh waters: ecological effects, interactions with other stressors, and prospects for the future. *Freshwater Biology* 55:152–174.

Vitousek, P. M., C. M. D'Antonio, L. L. Loope, M. Rejmánek, and R. Westbrooks. 1997. Introduced species: a significant component of human caused global change. *New Zealand Journal of Ecology* 21:1–16.

Ward, R. C., and C. A. Peters. 2003. Seeking a common framework for water quality monitoring. *Water Resources Impact* 5:3–7. (Note: The entire issue is devoted to a description of the monitoring framework.)

NPS 960/108554, July 2011